# MEMOIR OF A SOUL

## In Poetry and Prose

by Richard Heinz

## Acknowledgements

Many thanks to Amy Payne who first encouraged me to do more with my writing; to Ana Manwaring whose writing class provided a safe place to receive feedback on what I had written and whose editing skills helped refine my work. I'm grateful to Marcia Davis, and Rev. Janet Garvey-Spanvik, friends who took the time to read my drafts and provide extensive, specific suggestions for improvement. Finally, I offer love and gratitude to my family: Lynn who in our 35 years of marriage helped me to understand what it means to be truly intimate, Josh whose presence opened my soul to grace and Jennifer whose honest characterization of early drafts as "intellectual crap" caused me to go deeper than I thought possible.

----------------------------------------------------------------------------------

First Edition
September 2014

------------------

REH Publishing
Napa, CA 94558
email: rehpubs@sbcglobal.net

------------------

------------------

The events described in these pages are true, but all names have been changed to protect the privacy of individuals.

------------------

ISBN:
13:978-0692280645

# Introduction

I am an ordinary man living an ordinary life with one possible exception—the inner muse that gives voice to poems for me to record. The muse and the voice are infrequent visitors, but over a period of 35 years, they have left me with a collection of poems that come from my soul, a place I normally find difficult to visit. I say they come from my soul because they seem to reside at the intersection of my spiritual life and my all too human psychological life. What is my soul if not the joining of the human and the divine at the very center of my being?

In an effort to better understand what these poems were telling me, I explored each poem's meaning in a narrative reflection, creating a story of my life as experienced within my soul. As I read the results of my efforts, a number of themes emerged:

1. The innocence of childhood
2. My shadow side
3. My inward journey
4. Soulful connection
5. Beyond the curtain.

I have organized the poems and reflections in this book around those themes.

Several poems refer to childhood memories and moments when I first encountered my soul. Those experiences remain with me to this day, providing a stable foundation for my adult life.

It has been my experience that the innocent soul of the child can be buried by the pressures of socialization as we learn to modify our behavior and even our thoughts, in order to access the benefits of being an accepted member of society. This process may leave us with a sense of unworthiness at our core, creating a shadow side that follows us through life, repeatedly emerging and causing problems for us in our relationships.

I have found that when I embrace my shadow side, recognize it, call it by name and truly own it, I embrace my humanity. Authentic self-acceptance breaks down the defensive barriers that separate me from others, enabling the true human connection that brings joy.

The spiritual journey away from my shadow side and back to my true self is actually two parallel journeys. The first is an inward journey, centered on the struggle to move from ignorance of my shadow side to self-awareness, self-acceptance and self-love. Self-love of the soul is not self-involved as commonly understood in Greek mythology's story of Narcissus. Rather, it is a self-love that frees me to focus on others with love.

Although I still struggle with this inward journey, the process has provided me with a glimpse into a destination that lies beyond self love and is arrived at by only the most enlightened of souls—personal transformation. In its most powerful form, personal transformation brings a radical departure from a life lived out of a framework where self is the focus or center of our experience into a life lived from a paradigm of personal wholeness and authenticity, one where our framework is a unity or oneness with all creation. In her book *My Stroke Of Insight*, author Jill Bolte Taylor describes her own experience with this perspective of oneness. I find the concept of oneness important as I reflect upon highly spiritual beings such as Jesus, Buddha, Mohammed and Gandhi and try to understand their message for humanity.

The second journey is outwardly focused. Call it soulful connection. This is the joy of knowing we are not alone and that we have a deep spiritual connection with other souls, with creation and with the Creator. We understand at our core that we are an integral part of the wonder of creation and that creation itself is an act of love. As part of that creation, we ourselves are loved.

Our desire for soulful connection with other human beings is frequently expressed in the words *I need you* and their mirror image, _____ *needs me.* To need and be needed, as well as a desire to know and be known, are essential to a soulful life experience. Expressing the need for another person requires vulnerability. To know and be known allows others to see our frailties as well as our strengths. Vulnerability is an act of courage that opens the heart for nurturing love and mutual compassion.

In her book, *Daring Greatly*, Brené Brown's studies reveal that the single most important predictor of personal happiness is one's willingness to be vulnerable. Vulnerability is the key to soulful, personal connection.

These two spiritual journeys, inwardly and outwardly focused, lie at the center of the teachings of the world's great religions. Exemplified by the call to *love thy neighbor as thyself,* love of self and love of one's neighbor are inextricably linked in the human soul.

Finally, at the end of life we are ultimately alone in human terms trying to divine what lies in store for our souls beyond the curtain. Death is truly life's last great adventure.

Accessing the muse of my soul is difficult, as its voice lies hidden under a protective cover of ego with all its defenses and rationalizations. When I break through that protective cover I can experience my soul. Breakthroughs can occur under circumstances that vary widely. I know I am in touch with my soul when deep in my gut, I develop a sense of absolute certainty that I am good, loveable, loved and part of the wonder of creation. To me, my soul feels like the nucleus of an atom, a nugget of goodness and love that exists at my very core.

Being in touch with my soul liberates me from all the stresses of life that, in hindsight, are the stresses that limit my personal power and success. This stress relief often releases inexplicable creative energies, which, in my case, express themselves through poetry.

I can also experience my soul in sadness and emotional pain. Fear of emotional pain is a topic that appears throughout this book. Fear generally acts as a barrier to accessing our souls when we allow it to control our lives; but fear can also point the direction in which we need to move to experience our soul more fully. By moving toward our fear, by knowing it and embracing it, we disarm it and eliminate it as a barrier to the soul.

Although I don't feel joyful or comforted under conditions of sadness and pain, the experience can be just as fruitful as I gain a true understanding of loss and what it means to me. And, yes, pain can deepen my experience of life, opening my soul to a greater richness of human connection. Kahlil Gibran wrote of this in his book *The Prophet: "Your pain is the breaking of the shell that encloses your understanding."* True compassion requires a shared experience of pain and suffering.

Whatever shape the connection with our soul takes, it reflects an authentic, visceral and mystical experience of our true selves that cannot be explained. The circumstances leading to an experience can be told as can the feelings the experience engenders. But the origin of the experience remains a mystery.

Much of what I write in this book is highly personal. On one hand, I shudder at the audacity of thinking my intimate experiences and thoughts would be of interest to others. On the other hand, I share these intimacies in the hope that they will inspire your own personal growth and transformation. Henri Nouwen believed that what is most personal is most universal and that *by giving words to these intimate experiences, I can make my life available to others.* Because of the highly personal nature of what I have written, I have chosen to remain anonymous, not to protect myself, but to honor the privacy of those close to me who inevitably are part of my life story. For this reason all names in this book are fictional.

By exploring the potential of spiritual growth to be gained by journeying into the soul, I encourage you to venture into new realms of your own personal essence. Grounded in our essence, I believe we will all be better off as individuals and as a human society. It is in our essence that we know we are loveable and loved, the starting point for truly loving others.

# Recommendations for Readers

This book is a series of poems paired with personal reflections, explorations of what each poem meant to me, the poet. The poems are presented in a sequence that reflects my personal spiritual journey from the innocence of childhood to entering the final stages of my life, the actual ebbs and flows experienced in an ordinary life.

Rather than attempting to read the booklet straight through, I'd advise readers to begin by reading an individual poem. Take time to consider what it means for you, and then read the reflection. Before moving on to the next poem, I encourage you to write any thoughts in the blank space provided at the end of each section. You may find it helpful to refer to the appendix where I have included a number of questions that may stimulate your thinking about each section.

It is up to you how quickly you proceed to the next poem or section. I have found that the longer I stay with one pairing, the deeper my thinking and the more rewarding the final result.

I hope you will enjoy the journey.

# Order of Poems

## The Innocence of Childhood
1. The Child Within
2. The Wheat Field

## My Shadow Side
3. The Shadow
4. Hard Hearted
5. Jive'n 'n Strive'n

## My Inward Journey
6. Soaring
7. Nirvana's Gate
8. Grace

## Soulful Connection
9. My Boy
10. To Jennifer
11. Footsteps
12. Words
13. Soul Mates

## Beyond The Curtain
14. Alone
15. I Am
16. The Piper

## The Innocence of Childhood

1. The Child Within
2. The Wheat Field

## The Child Within

He is there, a tiny spec of human clay
Playing in the earth that forms his inner self,
A wander in his soul to go among the rest
And put his light to test.

I sit down beside him, he seems so small,
Until I see his eyes and know that all is well.
Not a word is spoken as we look upon each other,
Mingling souls in the liquid of our eyes.

He climbs up on my lap to comfort me
And says "Remember me forever" and "Let's go Daddy".
The world is safe when we're together
The child is guardian to the man.

# The Child Within

*Through our own recovered innocence we discern the
innocence of our neighbors*
— Henry David Thoreau

There is something natural about digging in the earth and
moving it so that it does what we want it to do. As if earth
is there to serve us, to help us and to protect us, all we
have to do is move it to where we want it. The earth
provides a sense of connection, a sense of being part of
something larger, of belonging. Maybe this is what we
mean when we talk about being grounded.

I find both of these thoughts very comforting. Yes,
I am part of something larger, and in belonging, I am
accepted just as I am. The world of humans does not
easily offer this sense of acceptance, but the earth does.

In moving the earth to reflect my will, I gain a
sense of power, a sense that I can influence what happens
to me. I can improve my circumstances as well as improve
the world around me.

I remember clearly one spring day when I was
four. The sun shone warmly, the air felt a bit cool, but
there was that hint of new life that raises our hopes after
a long cold winter. Someone had started to build a house
in the vacant lot next to where we lived in a suburban
neighborhood of rented duplexes. The construction crew
had left a pile of dirt from excavating the cellar.

I was playing in the dirt pile using my toy steam
shovel to scoop up the earth, put it into one of my toy
dump trucks and haul it to a place where I was making a
new pile. Anyone who has parented a young boy knows
that boys can continue happily in this kind of activity for

hours. All I know is that it fed some need in me and comforted me. Time had no meaning.

Then, I remember, I paused in my play and looked around. There was a tractor off in the distance plowing a field in preparation for spring planting. I felt the warmth of the sun and sensed the promise of new life bursting forth. I knew there was a bigger world out there, a friendly world, a world I wanted to explore, a world I could help shape in ways I couldn't even imagine. But I knew it was good.

I'm at the other end of life now. I know, or think I know, a lot more about the world and how it works. It's not always the friendly place I had imagined that spring day. But when I get discouraged about the world and all its troubles, I go back to that dirt pile and visit the little boy. I remember the moment when the world was good, when I knew I belonged, when I knew I could do great things. And I am renewed. The child truly is guardian to the man.

## The Wheat Field

Shades of gold shift in the wind,
nature's shimmer on a sea of grain.
Swaying stalks sigh in pianissimo,
in rhythm with the breeze.
White puffy clouds play with the sun,
inviting me to their dance.
Faint buzzing, life moving to its own rhythm,
eating, resting and reproducing.

I look for the stone
hidden between the rows,
my secret place.
Wading into that sea, rising to my chest
I move slowly,
careful not to bend a single stalk
lest others find
I have passed through here.

I lie down
face to the sun.
Earth cradles me
Wheat enfolds me
Sun warms me
Clouds entertain me.

I know I belong,
I am part of this wonder-
I am loved.

# The Wheat Field

*We are not human beings having a spiritual experience. We are spiritual beings having a human experience.*
-- Pierre Teilhard de Chardin

At age five, we moved to a house in a newly created housing development. When we moved in, and for several years thereafter, fields of wheat nearly surrounded the house. In a time before TV, we were left to our own devices to find ways to entertain ourselves in the fields and on the nearby farms.

As the grain grew and matured, we found great delight in creating small hiding places amidst the wheat where we could lie down and be completely unseen by anyone looking for us from the edge of the field. For a young child, being hidden from others brought a sense of excitement, maybe even a sense of power. Anyone who has played hide and seek as a child knows that kind of *I know something you don't know* excitement.

But another feeling stayed with me from hiding in that wheat. As I lay there looking up at the sun and clouds, I experienced a sense of peace, of safety and of wonder, as if I were an infant swaddled in blankets in my mother's arms.

The solid ground beneath my back gave a sense of security. I had nowhere to fall. The wheat enfolded me, much like the walls of a crib or cradle enfold a small baby. The sun warmed me like a heat lamp from a neonatal care unit. And the clouds, with their constantly changing shapes and patterns of white and gray, entertained me and engaged my imagination as I looked for new shapes and forms much as an infant looks in wonder at the toys hanging over his crib.

I don't believe those feelings signified a desire to return to the simple security of infancy, although that is certainly a possibility. Rather, I believe I wanted to capture and renew that sense of security, of belonging and wonder I experienced at the core of my being. I wanted to carry the feeling with me as I returned to the world outside the wheat field.

Even today, when I go back to the wheat field in my imagination, I come away reassured by the sense that I belong. I am part of the wonder of creation and I am loved. It is my experience that these simple, but fundamental, feelings constitute the very foundation for who I am as a human being. Without this foundation, my soul is set adrift to be buffeted by the pressures and uncertainties of human society. A soul adrift is a soul concerned with its own survival. There is less room for love, be it love of self or of others. But anchored to the foundation of inner knowing that I belong and I am loved, my soul is free to experience love to its fullest and to spread the joy of that experience to other souls. This is why I am here.

# Thoughts On The Innocence
## Of Childhood

## My Shadow Side

1. The Shadow
2. Hard Hearted
3. Jive'n 'n Strive'n

# The Shadow

There is a shadow deep within
Some, I suppose, would call it sin
But it is real and part of me
Hidden away where no one can see,
not even me.

And like water freezing in a crack
Splits a rock down its back
The shadow slowly pries apart
The relations dearest to my heart.

The shadow brings a sense of fear
The reason is not entirely clear
Until I gain a sense of trust
That I can handle what I must.

I have that choice to leave it there
Undisturbed, like Reagan's hair,
Hoping it will go away
But knowing it is here to stay.

What price I pay in withered soul
By failing to confront this darkened ghoul
But lurking deep within my mind
Lies a fear of what I will find.

And so I must enter that place
Where the shadow wields its mace
To battle the demon that shrinks my soul
So that I may be made truly whole.

And if I should lose that fight
Let them know there is no might
As long as the shadow stays inside
The soul is forced to forever hide.

But what if, instead of a mace,
I enter in with a simple embrace
And invite the shadow into the light
Sparing us both a costly fight?

After all, I know him not
And can't assume he's entirely rot
Perhaps he's afraid of me
Afraid of what I will see.

Perhaps he's tired of the dark
Hiding from my angry heart
And wants no more to fight the fight
But would welcome an invite to the light.

What is love that can't extend
A gracious welcome, loving hand
To the part of me I know
Is not the me I want to show.

But me it is in all its pain
Ugly me and full of shame
It needs my love to reunite
With my soul in the light.

Only when I am truly whole
Can I live fully from my soul
Only then can I truly love
And know my creator up above.

# The Shadow

*Compassion is not a relationship between the healer and the wounded. It's a relationship between equals. Only when we know our own darkness well can we be present with the darkness of others. Compassion becomes real when we recognize our shared humanity.*
— Pema Chodron, as quoted in *Daring Greatly* by Brené Brown

In a movie entitled *The Shadow*, The Shadow is a kind of superhero, able to slip through the tiniest crack in his pursuit of evil-doers. We all have our shadow that lives inside our psyche, but rather than a super hero, our shadow generally reflects personality traits and insecurities we would just as soon keep hidden from others because they reflect poorly on us. It is our shadow side that creeps into our most intimate relationships, creating problems that keep us from realizing our hopes and dreams in areas of utmost importance to us. Fear of discovery of our shadow side prevents authenticity in our lives, the authenticity that is necessary for true, loving relationship.

For much of my life, I was either unaware of my shadow side or unwilling to recognize its existence. This of course prevented me from dealing with my unproductive behaviors. In one sense this kept me feeling safe, because it kept people at a distance where, I thought, they could not see my inadequacies and vulnerabilities. At the same time, this distance prevented me from obtaining what was most important to me, a feeling of loving connection with others and with the world.

For clarification, I will describe my shadow side as a deeply held sense of insecurity about my abilities and my own self worth. Those who know me would probably wonder at that description. To most of the world I project an image of confidence and ability, And there is validity to this image. I am capable and I can be confident.

However, in an atmosphere of pressure, intimidation, judgment or over long periods of time, this image can fall apart, allowing my shadow side to emerge. I can become weak, indecisive and even passive. To avoid showing that side of me, I may assume a defensive and/or combative posture depending on the situation.

Although my defensive/ combative behavior can create problems in my relations with others, that is not the most destructive consequence of my shadow. Deep in my psyche I am not sure which is the real me. Am I capable or am I not? My shadow causes me to keep people at a distance where they cannot see my weak, indecisive and passive self.

It is interesting to explore the roots of my shadow side. When I was young, from age three to five, I was an out of control little boy. In kindergarten, the school psychologist designated me a "problem child." My offenses included biting the female principal in the leg, bullying other children and breaking my Sunday school teacher's glasses when I punched him in the face.

In the summer between kindergarten and first grade we moved to a new house served by a different elementary school. This school had a male principal, Dr. Boucher. Apparently my behavior continued to be unacceptable to the point where, several months into the school year, I was called into Dr. Boucher's office. As I sat down in a chair across the desk from the principal, I noticed a large wooden paddle lying on his desk. Dr. Boucher proceeded to explain that I had a decision to make. I could continue my bad behavior in which case he would be forced to use the paddle until I saw the error of my ways or I could *get with the program* and avoid something *neither of us really wanted.* I don't remember if he elaborated on the possible "carrot" side of the bargain, but in the weeks that followed, I found every good behavior recognized and rewarded with praise and special privileges.

I distinctly remember my 6th birthday, which occurred in December. My father dropped me off at my school about fifteen minutes after classes had started. As I walked up the driveway to the school, I remember thinking to myself, "Dick, its time to grow up and get with the program." It was a decision made consciously, willingly and without any sense of coercion. Thus began my socialization and the distancing from my true self. It was also the birth of my shadow side as I put my authentic self aside in order to pursue the rewards of society. From that point forward, I measured myself against the standards set by others without having understood or dealt with the underlying reasons for the anger that lay behind my bad behavior. This failure left me with a sense that my real self was not acceptable in some way. Measuring myself against standards set by others left me with a deep sense of insecurity.

Only as I began to truly experience life lived from and through my soul, did I recognize my shadow and the role it played in keeping others at a distance. I looked back on my life and saw the wreckage my shadow had left in its wake, the missed opportunities, the solitariness, the failures in my work life, and fractures in my intimate relationships. When I compared that to the love I felt in my more soulful relationships, I was unhappy, to say the least, knowing what my life could have been.

Of course, it's never too late to change and try to correct the mistakes I have made. I can also move forward with a new, more open approach to life. Success in these endeavors requires fundamental change on my part, not the destruction of my shadow, but embracing of my shadow, owning it, recognizing it and even coming to love it. It is part of me.

I don't want to give my shadow the power it had over my life previously, but I also recognize I cannot destroy it without destroying my essence, my soul. Embracing my shadow will rob it of its power, rendering it harmless. Without a doubt, it will reappear from time to time, but being conscious of its existence, will allow me to recognize it, acknowledge it and move on without giving it the power it once had. This, of course, requires that others may see my shadow side with all its imperfections. This is the risk I accept for living an authentic, soulful life.

## Hard Hearted

Oh, its a hardened heart I have
Remnant of my distant past
Evidence of struggles to find
Safety from anger's raging blast.

Oh, its a hardened heart I have
Forged in the heat of anger's flame
Caused by my unknowing act
And by her need to place the blame.

Oh, its a hardened heart I have
That feels the need to fire back
To show her that the path she chose
Does not bring her what she lacks.

Oh, its a hardened heart I have
That keeps me from love's deep rewards
How I wish I could recall
Harsh words flung in clashing chords.

I vaguely sense another way
A heart attuned to what she needs
Clear in mind , but far from heart
Where I need to plant the seed.

Compassion seems a simple thing
Natural, rational and all of that
Until the actual moment comes
When anger demands a tit for tat.

And if I master anger's steed
And find the compassion that meets her need,
Will she truly understand
That it is not me her anger feeds?

But then I guess I'll never know
Until I risk compassion's way
And trust that she will understand
My love is truly here to stay.

# Hard Hearted

*Anger is an acid that can do more harm to the vessel in which it is stored than to anything on which it is poured.*
—Mark Twain

*The flower fulfills its immanence, intelligence implicit in its unfolding. There is a discipline. The flower grows without mistakes. A man must grow himself, until he understands the intelligence of the flower.*
—From *The Snow Leopard* by: Peter Matthiessen

I have a problem dealing with anger in others, especially women with whom I am close. Unfortunately my relationship with Lynn, my wife for 35 years, was fraught with anger, which often blindsided me when I was least expecting it. There were long periods of time when I felt I was living in a minefield, never knowing when I was going to take the step that set off an explosion of anger and, on occasion, rage. Although I truly loved Lynn and recognized that there were many periods of joy and family harmony, after 35 years, the fear and stress of unresolved anger on both our parts finally led to divorce.

In fairness to Lynn, I need to insert a caveat here. My perception of her anger has as much to do with me and my own history as it has to do with Lynn. There was no neutral third party observing our relationship, advising us as to whose anger or response was outside the boundaries of a "normal" marital relationship. As in most relationships, I believe our inability to get along was due to personality traits that lay deep within both our psyches. My intention here is not to place blame but rather, to explore the corrosive role anger can play in a relationship.

If my childhood had been different, I might have been better prepared to cope with Lynn's anger. My earliest memory is of me as a very small child standing, looking up at my mother who is obviously very angry with me. Her right hand is raised, and in that hand she holds a large wooden spoon, her instrument of choice when it came to punishment. I am about to receive that punishment and there is nothing I can do about it. But I distinctly remember thinking, *you can have my body but you can't have me*. That *me* was my essential self, separate from my physical self. Today, I would call it my soul.

With a lifetime of experience to draw from, it is clear that that one pivotal moment with my mother was an epochal turning point in my psychological development. A singular event influenced many years to follow, particularly in dealing with authority figures and in dealing with anger, especially anger in women.

And no, I don't hold my mother responsible for my problems. As a parent, I recognize that parenting is not easy and that we all make many mistakes. Seemingly insignificant interactions can have an outsized effect on a child unbeknownst to the parent. It is up to the child, as an adult, to understand the unproductive coping mechanisms developed in childhood and deal with those behaviors as an adult.

True forgiveness is always a good first step. After my early childhood years, my mother and I developed a close relationship in which I experienced nothing but love, kindness and wisdom from her until she died peacefully at age 96. That is how I remember my mother and will continue to hold her in my heart.

If I go back in my mind and relive that moment of anger with my mother, I find it helpful to refocus my inner camera away from the anger I felt towards my mother and, instead, focus on the reason I felt that anger. When I do this, I find the little boy crying out, *I am not bad. I am good!* At my very core, I imagine a glowing, solid mass of what I can only call Goodness. I am struck with an overwhelming sense that I am Goodness and that I am deserving of love because I am good. When I ask, what is Goodness? The answer immediately comes: Goodness is love, plus acts of love. That is my essential self; that is my soul.

When I refocus on that moment with my mother, I find my outrage at the injustice has dissolved, replaced with the knowledge that my mother did not understand. She didn't know that glowing, solid mass of Goodness that is the essential me. She was, as I am, human.

Lest I create the impression that my early childhood was difficult and unhappy, I need to say that it wasn't. There were many times, especially in nature, when that little boy experienced his soul embraced by a sense of belonging, of being part of the wonder of creation and of being loved. These experiences and the memory of the comfort they brought, have stayed with me throughout my life, providing a refuge where I can retreat and find renewal.

Unfortunately the lessons I learned from childhood were not helpful in dealing with my marital relationship. The first lesson I learned as a small child was that I could punish my mother by withholding myself from her. I also learned not to reward displays of anger by giving in to their demands. Both responses are hard-hearted, totally lacking in love and compassion.

The poem is not entirely clear about where the anger lies. Is it anger within the poet or is it anger directed at the poet? Although written with the latter in mind, I find it interesting that it can be read from either point of view. Anger wreaks the most harm when it's not in one person, but in both. Both parties are on autopilot, driven by ghosts of experiences from years past.

Despite what they think, neither party is in control of his or her own emotions and attitudes.

Multiple layers and sources of anger make it difficult to dispel, since the stated reasons for the anger are not the real drivers behind the emotions. The underlying catalyst may be buried deep within the psyche of the participants. In my case, my response to Lynn's anger often had its source in my unresolved anger with my mother and her wooden spoon. Likewise Lynn had issues of her own having grown up in an alcoholic family. Any argument between the two of us was driven to a large degree by unresolved issues from the past. The real issues often remained beneath the surface, unacknowledged, making resolution impossible.

There is hope. Lynn and I still need to interact, especially around issues having to do with our adult, special-needs son. We are moving beyond recrimination to friendship. On those rare occasions when I find my anger rising in response to something she has said or done, I have been able to catch myself, recognize what is happening and choose to respond in a way that is constructive. Maybe the emotional distance created by divorce has allowed me to feel less threatened by her. But then again, perhaps I'm making progress in handling anger.

# Jive'n 'n Strive'n

Little Me shucks
And Little Me jives
Little Me thrives
Just stay'n alive.

Big Me ducks
And Big Me covers
Big Me hides
While Little Me hovers.

That ain't no way
To be yo'self
Where's your pride
When you're doin the hide?

Who dat man
You thinks you is
When you can't come out
Without that pout?

What you doin
Runin away
From the love life sends
Along your way?

Get your ass
Back'n the game
That Big Me fella
Gonna make me a name.

Stand'n up tall
Take'n it all
Big Me loves
In spite of it all.

Big Me shows
That he's the one
That they'll remember
When all is done.

# Jive'n 'n Strive'n

*How much pain they have cost us, the evils that have never happened.*
—Thomas Jefferson

A good friend and teacher of creative writing advised me to alter the language of this poem because the use of African-American vernacular may be perceived as racist. I certainly don't want to be seen as racist nor do I want to offend anyone by the language I use. Nevertheless, I was intrigued as to why this poem came to me in a lexicon so unlike any of my other poems, and I wanted to explore it.

I was reminded of a dream I once had where the main character, a black man, did some pretty horrible things. My therapist at the time pointed out that when a black person appears in dreams of a white person, the black person often symbolizes the dreamer himself or a close relation. The dreamer needs to disguise the main character's identity because his behavior is something he doesn't want to recognize in himself or in his close relation. Given the subject of this poem, it seemed that linguistically, I was doing what I had done in my dream, disguising my dark side, my "Little Me," because I didn't want to recognize and own that part of me.

I believe we all have our Big Me and our Little Me. Our Big Me is the authentic self, the self that wants to do the right thing, take the high road, the self that is genuinely concerned for others. Big Me can do all these things because he is secure in the knowledge that he is loved and worthy of being loved.

But our Little Me is also there, constantly reminding us of the dangers in the world, of the wrongs done to us, and the evils lurking in the hearts and minds of others. He also reminds us of all the mistakes we have made in the past and suggests that we are not really worthy of being loved.

Little Me is an aggressive fellow, often urging us to head off dangers he sees in our world. He projects motives and characteristics onto others that allow us to justify actions against the other person. He wants to keep others at a distance so they can not see just how bad, incompetent and unlovable we really are.

One can draw an interesting analogy between Big Me, Little Me and the story of David and Goliath. Goliath views the world through a lens that sees only that which he values. His is a world where physical aggression, raw power, weapons and armor are keys to success. His is the world of Little Me. It is also the world in which many of us reside, often referred to as "the real world".

David on the other hand, is armed only with a sling, a pebble and faith in the power of God. David's faith is like a channel through which the power of the Creator flows to assist him in his moment of need. This is the world of Big Me, simple, focused and internally at peace in the knowledge that his is the real power in the world.

Many of us, myself included, choose to see the world through the eyes of Little Me. We have no trouble finding evidence of how the "real world" works. We choose to live by the rules of this world because it is tangible and easier for us to understand. The world of Big Me seems hazy, undefined, difficult to enter and high-risk.

In my own life, I would describe my Little Me as that part of me that lacks generosity in both material and emotional areas. I can be ungenerous materially because I fear I may someday run out of money and I need to keep enough to satisfy my rainy-day needs. This fear exists in spite of the fact that by most people's standards, I have more than my fair share of wealth.

Disagreement over money was a recurring theme in my marriage. By nature, Lynn was optimistic, celebratory of life and always looking for new projects to start, all admirable characteristics. From my vantage point, however, she paid relatively little attention to the financial impact of her desires. Perhaps she depended on my tight-fisted mentality to make sure we didn't go too far. Many couples share a similar dynamic, where one person is more prone to spending, the other to saving. If this dynamic is not moderated by a sense of cooperation and understanding, it can lead to each partner becoming one-dimensional in the relationship, always playing the same role and becoming something of a caricature in the mind of the other.

I am emotionally ungenerous when I focus on my own emotions of fear and a sense of unworthiness. I don't have the energy to concern myself with the emotions of others. Little Me tells me their emotions are their problem to deal with. My Little Me lacks empathy. I convince myself that people wind up in difficult situations because it is their own fault, or the result of fate rolling the dice with an unfortunate result. "That's life," or so says Little Me.

To me, and I suspect to many others, it often feels as if I live in a war zone. And like an actual war zone, stress builds and builds until someday, I suffer from a form of PTSD. At that point, I either make constructive changes or I decide to cope by burying all my feelings in a coffin of denial. In the latter case, I continue on with my life, often with reasonable success, unaware of what I am missing, unaware of the richness that comes from the freedom to live from my authentic self. Sooner or later I may even lose contact with Big Me as I give Little Me complete control over my life.

I can change. I can dethrone Little Me and take my life back, putting Big Me back in charge. Bringing Big Me back can be a joyful event as I recognize the beauty that is my true self.

I am reminded of the Biblical story of the prodigal son and the joy felt by the father as he welcomes back the son whom he had lost to the life of a Little Me. The prodigal son returns with no demands or expectations other than to be allowed to do the lowliest of tasks in return for some shelter and food. The older brother, of course, remaining firmly in his Little Me role, sees nothing but unfairness and threat of losing his father's love.

Perhaps this story is as much about our need to reclaim our Big Me as we age and our need to forgive ourselves without condition as it is about a father's relationship with his sons. We can never totally free ourselves from our Little Me. All we can do is take away his power, not by doing battle with him, but by recognizing him, forgiving him and welcoming him back into the family, albeit in a very limited role.

# Thoughts On My Shadow Side

## My Inward Journey

1. Soaring
2. Nirvana's Gate
3. Grace

## Soaring

A peacock feathered eagle
Soaring on the power of his soul,
A bird of prey, at one with his world,
Neither hate nor pity nor love nor guilt exist
As he searches out the one his birthright makes
His dinner for a day.

A simple life, his place is certain.
Rock solid sure and undisturbed
By thoughts or doubts of human making
He soars on currents made for his taking.

Can we achieve that sense of peace
That comes from total faith in One
Who rules our world from above
Who hopes we'll soar and know His love?

# Soaring

*There is an eagle in me that wants to soar, and there is a*
*hippopotamus in me that wants to wallow in the mud.*
—Carl Sandburg

In 1987, I took a thirteen-week sabbatical from my job in a high
tech company. Much of this sabbatical was spent traveling
through the Northern Rockies in an RV with my wife and two
young children. With plenty of time, there was no pressure to
hurry from one activity to another so everyone could be satisfied.
It was truly a stress-relieving experience.

For the thirteenth week, I left the family at home and
went to Esalen, a retreat center on the Big Sur coast of California,
for a week of yoga and meditation. At one point in the course, we
were given peacock feathers and left to do whatever we wanted
while some music played. I began to mentally "fly" around the
room and soon found myself soaring over the canyon of the
Yellowstone, which we had visited a few weeks before.

I soared and floated on the currents as I looked down to
see if a meal might present itself. I had an overwhelming feeling
of belonging. I felt completely at peace. Any feeling of separation
was replaced by knowing that I was part of something, that I
belonged and that it was good. The beauty of the canyon from
1000 feet up, the freedom of soaring wherever I wanted to go,
the sense of belonging, all combined to create a sense of peace
that said all was right with me and with the world.

On one level, the poem suggests that a lack of emotion is
equated with the peaceful state we seek. The hunt for food
elicited no emotion. I didn't need to hate my quarry, pity it or
feel guilty about taking its life. It just was. It was, as I was, part of
the oneness and continuum that made life possible. Life itself is

good and must be continued. One way or another, we all serve to continue life.

Of course I have to wonder what my potential dinner was feeling. After all, the eagle is at the top of the food chain and has relatively little to fear in the world. But we've all seen those quivering ground squirrels sitting beside their burrow constantly scanning for danger. No sense of peace there.

Both the ground squirrel and the eagle will die sooner or later, but the squirrel is acutely aware that sooner is a real possibility if he is not alert to danger. That's where I seem to live much of the time, not fearing for my physical life but fearing I will be separated from things that I value.

Some things are especially vulnerable to loss such as my job, my wealth, my status, my whole way of life. However, on closer examination, the fears that most affect my happiness are those that result from the tension, irritation, resentment and anger that sometimes appear in my relationships.

In my relationships I am most vulnerable and most fearful of being hurt. Hence, my sensitivity increases when I perceive slights, put downs or anger directed towards me. When I feel threatened in this way, I often retreat into an emotional burrow, refusing to venture out until I am sure the danger is gone. And like the ground squirrel, the more times I encounter danger, the closer I stay to my burrow. With time, my life becomes more and more constricted to a small, emotionally-safe territory. I avoid topics of conversation I perceive as risky. Similarly, I refuse to even try some activities with the potential for failure, embarrassment or friction with a loved one.

It is interesting that the eagle soars on currents of air that are invisible to him. Yet he launches himself into space, having faith that the air under his wings will support him. The ground squirrel, on the other hand, is firmly tied to mother earth and the safety of his burrow. His support system is visible and tangible. But it is the ground squirrel that lives in constant fear.

Like the eagle, I am blessed with relative physical security, yet when it comes to my emotional life, I often choose to live as the ground squirrel. For me, this poem is an invitation to throw off the chains that keep me repeating the same old negative responses and limiting the richness of my emotional life. It's an invitation to launch myself into the void of feelings and emotional vulnerability, despite possible rejection, loss or failure. In risking, I am open to the possibility of empathy and understanding, in other words, true human connection. In soaring, I experience the richness of God's creation from a whole new perspective, a perspective of oneness and love.

## Nirvana's Gate

The truth is captured deep within
Lighting the inner reaches of my being
Where only I can release its power
To reach the glory of Nirvana's tower

Only I prevent the light
From bathing all I love
In health and beauty of
Serenity in my life.

What fear is so great
That I lock the gate
And deny myself the pleasures
Of a higher state?

A leap of faith
That I am might
Is  all I need to
See the light

An act of trust
In myself,
Is that so much
To keep me hushed?

Can I truly
Love myself?

# Nirvana's Gate

*Self love is the source of all our other loves.*
—Pierre Corneille

Jesus said, "Love thy neighbor as thyself." It sounds simple enough, but for those two little words "as thyself." In my life, feeling totally lovable and loved has been an extremely rare experience. But on those rare occasions when it did occur, believe me, it was a joyful, even ecstatic, experience. I knew in the core of my being that I was good, that the world was good and my soul was part of something larger, connected to all the souls of the world.

Feeling totally loved and loveable freed me from feeling separate from the world. To say that I loved others does not capture the feeling. It was more that I felt merged with the world. The sense of separateness that is implicit in any statement of love for another was totally missing. It was as if I had stepped through the looking glass and was able to experience the world from a new paradigm of oneness, a paradigm that was invisible to those around me.

And no, I was not on drugs. But I had just completed a five-day course of psychological exercises and meditations. I felt like someone had stuck a giant toothbrush down my throat and totally cleaned out all the gunk that blocked the path between my head and my gut. Negative emotions—fear, guilt, anger and competitiveness—all were gone. I was free to be me, the good me, the loveable me, the loving me. I was free to be totally present for and focused on those around me.

This wonderful, ecstatic experience lasted a couple of days. Then the old fears began to creep back in. The gate swung shut, my head disconnected from my gut and I resumed my previous life.

In her book, *My Stroke Of Insight*, Jill Bolte Taylor describes a similar experience, brought on by her cerebral hemorrhage. She felt her consciousness—her I AM, if you will, was everywhere and in everything all at the same time, as if she had become liquid . In her case, the experience lasted for months. Because she had to work to recover the functions of her damaged brain, she was able to consciously select those parts of her I AM she wanted to nurture.

I ask myself, why? Why did I not try to keep the experience alive? What did I fear?

I'm still not clear, but I believe that at one level I recognized that other human beings produced my experience. For me, this raised the question of trust. Did I fear putting myself in the hands of others who understood human psychology at a level beyond anything I would ever know?

On another level, I told myself I was unwilling to take the risk of turning my life upside down when I had a wife and child to support. I was afraid of what I would feel compelled to do if I followed the path I had come across. It was not just that I felt I could not be like Sidhartha, the Buddha, who left all that was precious to him in pursuit of spiritual enlightenment. Even if I pursued my spiritual quest while maintaining my current life in the world, I was afraid that success in pursuing the path would lead me to dissatisfaction with that life. I would no longer be content focusing my energies on the world of business. I was concerned that my changed values and priorities would have serious consequences for my closest relationships whose lives could be greatly impacted by my changes.

Change of any kind has the potential to create tensions in our lives as well as to bring new and exciting renewal. We all live with change and adapt to it with varying degrees of success. Transformational change, however, has far greater potential for upsetting the comforts we have created for ourselves, be they material or in our relationships.

In this case, I allowed my fear to create a narrative of all the problems that could arise by moving in the direction of change. I allowed my fear to close the door on even the possibility of pursuing change in small, incremental steps, at least to the point where I encountered real problems that might give cause to reconsider my decision. I allowed fear to make my decision.

So where does that leave me? On a personal level it leaves me with a deep sense of possibilities of what life could be like. At the deepest level of my consciousness, I know I am loveable and loved, but I still find it difficult to live from a place of total faith in that knowledge. I still experience my life largely through a lens of fear that masks that deeper knowledge and prevents me from living 100 percent from my authentic, loving and loveable self.

It is clear to me that unless I work at it every day and in every situation I face, the negatives in my life soon return to block any real change. Perhaps I am just too comfortable in my life to generate the energy and commitment needed to accomplish the kind of fundamental change I know is possible.

Finally, this experience greatly increases my faith in the messages brought to us in the Gospels. When I look at the New Testament through the lens of this experience, I see Jesus as a real human being, transformed by his experience at the baptism. Through baptism, he enters a new paradigm for existence. He understands the Kingdom of Heaven is available to each of us, and that we are all one. Knowing we are loved is the starting point for our own transformation.

To me, this is the challenge of our faith, to transform the world through love, one soul at a time, so we can all experience what Jesus was trying to show us, so humanity can live in peace and love forever. My personal challenge is to move through my fears in the faith that my transformed self will have the wisdom and power to deal with the consequences of my changes with love.

# Grace

No midnight swims in open ocean
No downhill runs through flying snow
No rows of badges of an Eagle scout
No natural leader with friends about

No winning goals
No pretty girls
No straight A reports
No letters in three sports

I feel the wishes welling up
That life had dealt a different hand
And given me a son
Blessed with achievements grand.

But then I see in my mind
A freckled face and adoring eyes
A joyful smile, a skipping step
Arms raised high in a victory lap.

What a gift to one like me
A heart too small to let me see
Until love brings a sense of grace
Through the power of a son's embrace.

# Grace

*I do not at all understand the mystery of grace- only that it meets us where we are but does not leave us where it found us.*
—Anne LaMott


My son Josh was born with significant learning disabilities. Although mainstreamed for much of his education, as a sports nut, he was more mascot than player. He gamely tried T-ball, pitching machine baseball and grade school basketball with decreasing success. But the coaches loved having him on the team. No one else could match the joy that Josh showed when he managed to make a play or sink a basket. At Josh's 8th grade graduation, his persistence and good nature were recognized. He received a coveted award for the most inspirational student in his class. However, in the years that followed, fewer and fewer classmates were willing to spend time with him.

Josh spent most of his high school years at a small private school for children with serious learning issues. However, approaching his senior year he rebelled and insisted on attending the local public high school at least half time so he could play sports. He wanted to play football but his cerebral shunt, not to mention his small size and lack of experience, said no way. The coach made Josh an equipment manager and, as something of a team mascot, Josh got to lead the team onto the field at the start of each game and at halftime. Running at full speed with arms raised in a victory salute, he led the team out. Josh's team won the local CCS championship that year.

Josh also joined the wrestling and lacrosse teams his senior year. He actually managed to win several wrestling matches because of his strength. In lacrosse, he loved to run into the opposing players, a move that soon became known as *joshalizing* the opponent. Catching the ball in the stick always remained a somewhat illusive skill, however. But again Josh's enthusiasm and desire proved contagious, demonstrating the true meaning of the term *for love of the game.*

I tell you this not to suggest that I, as Josh's father, deserve any credit for Josh's success. Like all parents, I've made many mistakes, especially when my own frustrations with Josh's abilities led me to say or do things hurtful to Josh.

In the end, it is not about what I taught Josh, but about what Josh has taught me. You see, I was one of those achievers growing up, a reasonably talented jock—good grades, class president, pretty girls and good colleges. Earlier in life, I thought this was what life was about, and I expected the same for my son. Josh saved me from all that.

Josh taught me about grace, the grace that allows me to meet another human being where they are, not where I want them to be. Grace that lets me see the value others bring to the world, even when it is something I wouldn't normally value. Grace that offers encouragement rather than judgment. Grace that gently reminds me to give up my own desires to meet the needs of another. Grace that nurtures rather than drives.

We can't have too much grace in this world. I still struggle to live up to the word, experiencing as many failures as successes. It can be discouraging. But when I do get it right, it's worth all the struggle or, as Josh would say, "It's a home run!"

# Thoughts On My Inward Journey

# Soulful Connection

1. My Boy
2. To Jennifer
3. Footsteps
4. Words
5. Soul Mates

## My Boy

God sent me the boy I need
A boy who loves
A boy who shares
Full of joy
A boy who cares.

God sent me a boy who needs me
To teach me to love
To teach me to share
To teach me joy
To teach me to care.

God needs me to be the one
To share his love
To share his joy
To be the one
To love his boy.

# My Boy

*In all our contacts it is probably the sense of being really needed and wanted that gives us the greatest satisfaction and creates the most lasting bond.*
–Eleanor Roosevelt

When Josh was in first grade, he played T-ball on a team with other first graders. For those unfamiliar with T-ball, it is baseball for beginners, where the ball is placed on a T for the batter to hit easily. Any adult who has experienced T-ball knows that it can be somewhat chaotic as kids try to learn the basics of the game, like which way to run, when to run and where to throw the ball.

As a T-baller, Josh experienced somewhat limited success. I did not pick up on his awareness of his relative lack of success until one game when he was assigned to play third base. Recognizing that Josh needed some extra coaching, I positioned myself near third base so I could help him understand what to do should a ball come his way. With runners on first and second, Josh told me very clearly that if a ball came his way, he would stop it, grab it, take it over and step on third base and then throw the ball to the catcher, which ends the play in T-ball. I affirmed his plan.

Low and behold, the batter hit a nice soft grounder right to Josh. He trapped the ball with his mitt, picked it up, trotted over to tag third base, and threw the ball to the catcher. He then looked up at me, a look of absolute joy on his face and said, " Dad, Dad, my team needs me!" He raised his arms in a victory salute and danced around in a celebratory circle, knowing he was a valued member of the team.

There wasn't an adult at the game who didn't share in Josh's joy. Perhaps they were wondering, as I was, when was the last time they had felt such unadulterated joy? And when was the last time they really felt needed in a way that could even hope to unleash such joy?

When Josh was in the 7th grade, he attended a Boy Scout summer camp and I went along as an adult supervisor. The camp bordered a small lake and every day the boys had swim time. All the boys could swim, except Josh. So while the other boys were diving and splashing and playing in the lake, Josh took a swimming lesson near the dock, close to shore.

I watched him from a safe distance. A skinny, shivering little kid, thrashing about in the water, clearly suggesting to me, at least, that he would never learn to swim that day or any other. But he kept trying, ever hopeful that something would change. Hoping that someday, with enough hard work, he would be just like the other boys.

That's when I knew what it is to be needed. I couldn't make Josh be like the other boys. I couldn't take away the disappointment and pain that Josh must have felt every day when he faced the reality of his capabilities. But I could feel his hopes and dreams as well as his pain and disappointment. I could hold those feelings and by doing so I could hold Josh. Josh needed someone to hold him and love him just the way he was. Josh needed me!

## To Jennifer

I was there when you were born.
What a joy it was to see
Those curious eyes
Looking up at me.

I looked back
What did I see?
A beautiful mind,
A soul that was free.

What a gift to one like me
A soul bound up in needless fears
Freed by the love
Shown in my tears.

As the years went by
We shared so much
Rides on my bike,
McDonalds for lunch.

But I should have remembered
How you cried
When at the end of the movie
Bambi's father died.

When a woman you became
I failed to make
The transition to
Your new found state.

I left you alone
With your wanting to say
'What have I done
To drive you away?'

Years have passed,
There's little to do
Except to say
"I'm sorry"
And "I love you."

## To Jennifer

*I can only hope that neither of my daughters was scarred by their upbringing.*
—Georg Solti

Jennifer was born an old soul. When the doctor handed her to me minutes after she was born, she looked up with a curious look that said *well, who are you?* There was no fear, no blank unknowing stare, no crying, just a sense of wonder at encountering something new.

As she grew older, Jennifer showed that solid emotional base that gave her a sense of well being at her core. She had unusual common sense as well as the ability to express herself in simple, straight-forward language, and an intelligence that brought simplicity to the most complex problems. Exhibiting a wicked sense of humor as well as an ability to draw, I wondered if she might become a stand-up comic or cartoonist. I could not have been more proud of Jennifer.

When Jennifer was four, my wife and I took her to see the movie Bambi. Jennifer sat through the forest fire, the hunt and even the death of Bambi's mother without uttering a peep. But the last scene of the movie shows the grown Bambi standing beside his father on a rock outcropping with the setting sun in the background. Signifying the passing of the torch to a new generation, Bambi's father turns and walks away into the sunset.

Suddenly Jennifer burst into tears, crying out that the father was leaving. I tried to console her, telling her that I was there with her and I would not be leaving. I knew then and should have remembered going forward, that as her father, I was a very important person to my daughter. Jennifer needed me.

Jennifer and I were close during her early years. On Saturdays, we would often go to lunch at McDonalds or some other favorite restaurant. Until she grew too big, I would carry her on a child seat on my bike to visit with her friends. As she grew older, I attended her sporting events to cheer her on and always let her know how well she did. On several occasions, we went backpacking together in the Sierra Nevada.

When Jennifer reached puberty, I found myself feeling awkward around her. Not that I was physically attracted to her, but I was now dealing with a different being—a young woman. She was becoming my equal, yet becoming different from me, as women are from men. I felt awkward and worried I might inadvertently do or say something that could be misinterpreted. I'm certain Jennifer felt my awkwardness and recognized the growing distance between us.

Not knowing what to do, I turned my parenting and nurturing energies increasingly toward Josh, who by necessity and perhaps by nature, could easily consume most of my parenting and emotional energy. It was natural and easy to be a nurturing parent to Josh because his needs were so great and so obvious. In some ways, Josh was the lucky one as I am sure Jennifer was hurt by my change in focus.

I should have remembered that just like her brother, Jennifer needed me. Even as a young woman she needed me to be close to her, supporting her and encouraging her. Most importantly, just like Josh, Jennifer needed me to show my love simply and naturally. But instead we grew further apart mainly due to my inattention.

Now that I am in my later years, I can see my mistakes and the consequences they brought. I would like to have a closer relationship with Jennifer, but years build habits and distances that are hard to overcome. We both try and yet I can't help but recognize a certain symmetry when I hear the call from deep within saying, *Jennifer, I need you.*

# Footsteps

Shuffling footsteps in midnight darkness
Bring to mind my own confusion
Frustration with an ebbing will
And memories of a loving fusion.

Aging father and midlife son
Bound together in life's unending cycle
The body fights its losing battle
The spirit follows inevitably after.

Its my turn now to extend a hand
To help him further down the trail
A gesture that can not repay
The debt I feel to my father frail.

I long to be in times gone by
Bearing what I know today
To share my thanks in active play
Enriching life in deep communion.

But wisdom comes too late in life
Out of synch with what we'd like
Actions fail the test of time
And words alone are left to bind.

I love you Dad for all you've been
Patiently helping me through life's din
When all is done and laid to rest
Its you, I know, gave your best.

# Footsteps

*We never know the love of a parent until we become parents ourselves.*
—Henry Ward Beecher

My Dad died at the age of 82 when I was 50 years old. He was a good man and a good father. He was kind, gentle, never cross and only occasionally impatient.

He and I were very different. He loved to work with his hands. I hated working with my hands but loved to read. Dad's reading extended to Popular Mechanics magazine. I was into sports while my Dad had never played sports and even as an adult could barely swim across the pool. Add to our natural differences the fact that he was busy for many years building the house in which we lived while I became a typical moody, remote teenager out of reach of even the most loving parent.

It was only as an adult, when I had my own family that we began to come together as friends. Dad was curious about my life and I was able to introduce him and my mother to interesting new experiences in San Francisco and the larger Northern California area. Still, as he approached the end of his life, I found it difficult to establish any kind of deep and meaningful conversation to thank him for all he had done for me.

I wrote this poem after one of his visits to our home. It came to me in the middle of the night, awakened by the sound of my father's footsteps shuffling in the hall as he made his way to the bathroom. Perhaps it was the frailty reflected in his shuffling walk that penetrated my consciousness and led me to realize that I was now the parent and he was the one who needed to be loved and supported. I knew then that I had missed so many opportunities to show my love and gratitude. I felt the loss and wished for a different history to our relationship.

It's strange, but as I age, I see more and more of my father in me, such as thought patterns, facial expressions, physical impairments, retreating from the world into the things that I love to do by myself. In some ways I feel closer to my father years after his death than I did when he was alive. It's also a bit unnerving. I always saw myself as surpassing my Dad in life, and in many ways I have, a fact that gave him great pride. But there seems to be little chance of escaping the destiny programmed into my genes.

# Words

The words, they come streaming forth
A gift from some unknown place
They let me know I am not alone
In this mass of the human race

The words, they free my buried soul
From all that hides its glowing light
Racing mind and anxious thoughts
Simple words put to flight

The words, they paint a picture in my heart
Of God's love in human form
Lighting the way  to know his grace
Lighting the way  to be reborn.

The words, they fade as fears they start
To enter the cracks in my heart
Racing mind and anxious thoughts
Leave my soul in the dark.

# Words

*Be still and know that I am God.*
—Psalm 46 verse 10

We've all experienced moments of creative inspiration when we suddenly see the simple answer to some complex problem we've puzzled over. The mind's ability to resolve complex questions into simple truths, is amazing and truly a mystery.

But there is another kind of creative inspiration that seems different in some fundamental way. It shows itself in works of art, music, poetry and prose. These works come from and speak to a different part of our being. Maybe it's the difference between our left and right brains but, if so, our two halves might as well be different worlds.

Writing poetry, for me, is a mysterious process. It's as if a poet were dictating the words to me, and my only task is to write them down. The words seem to exist totally apart from myself, disembodied if you will. But where do these words come from? Where is this poet? Why does he go away for long periods? How can I contact him?

I don't know the answers to these questions. I do know that he comes most often when I am in a place where my spirit is free of the everyday stresses and strains that occupy my mind most of my waking hours. As I age and my life simplifies, I am trying to make more space for this voice to enter.

I make this effort because I cherish those moments when this poet opens my soul to the world. He makes me human. He brings me to the truths of my own life. He shows me what could be. He lets me know that I am loved and able to love. I need the anchor he provides against the winds of life as they try to scatter me, a leaf in the autumn of life.

We all have our own concept of God. Mine is that God is the spirit that connects us all. Its as if individually, we are each a neuron in some greater intelligence called God. In the human brain, each individual neuron, on its own, is lacking in any kind of intelligence. It's only when the mass of neurons combines their efforts that coherent thoughts emerge. Perhaps we human beings are just that, individual neurons, which when working together with others, in God, unleash God's creative power acting through us. When we humans manage to tap into God's creative power, we too can create in ways we can't explain. Is that the poet I seek?

# Soul Mates

The glance, the smile, the unexpected touch,
The  laugh, the knowing look,
The double entendre shared only by us
Give reflection to the story within.

The music plays in our beating hearts
Synchronized by our common desire
We dance in circles that grow ever smaller
Bringing us closer to the glowing fire.

With eyes on the prize, our lips engage
Lightly at first, hinting at delights yet to come
A journey for two, merging spirit and joy
Into one soul, in a union of love.

What joy it brings to please my other
To free her from all earthly cares
If only for a moment of bliss
Ending silently with a gentle kiss.

# Soul Mates

*Love one another, but make not a bond of love: Let it rather be a moving sea between the shores of your souls.—*
Kahlil Gibran

I am very physical in my personal relationships with women. As a teenager, that was all I could think about, which is not unusual I suppose. But as I grew in my experience with intimacy, I realized it was the underlying emotional and spiritual connection with my partner that brought true satisfaction and joy to the union. The longer and subtler the process leading up to the union, the closer we became in spirit and the more satisfying became the ultimate physical joining.

I suspect that as a male, this appreciation of the spiritual side of intimacy had to be consciously nurtured in order to grow and flourish whereas for women it is a natural priority in relationships. Women seem to innately understand that spiritual and emotional connection cements the relationship and holds it together through the trials of time.

Like many things in my life, I have found that establishing the spiritual basis for physical intimacy is often difficult and can take conscious effort. This is in stark contrast to my fantasies that picture my partner and I organically communicating our mutual desire through unspoken, subtle communications.

In my fantasies, I picture my partner and I exchanging knowing looks, casual touches and secret meanings, all leading to a stronger and stronger mutual understanding of a shared desire. This mutual but unspoken understanding brings with it an excitement as I look to see how she will move the game forward in response to my latest signal.

I say fantasies because in my experience it has been difficult to achieve. My partner and I both lead busy lives. We come together at the end of the day or week full of stress and with personal agendas that may not be in synch. It takes conscious effort to make time to relax, clear our minds of all our stresses and to slowly rebuild the spiritual ties between us. The effort can seem like work if both parties are not consciously moving in the same direction. But when we do achieve that deep, soulful connection, it can create a memory that stays with us forever.

Although not an exact parallel to the poem, I can remember one time that has stayed with me over the years because of the spiritual connection it held. I was on a business trip to meet with a female sales rep. Over breakfast at my hotel, she informed me that the customer had postponed our appointment until the afternoon. I suggested we use the time to train on some new software I had on my computer. We went to my room and spent the next hour or so focused on the new material.

Both she and I were married, and although I had always found her attractive, the idea of starting a relationship with her never crossed my mind even after an hour or so alone in my room. Suddenly, I looked at her to see if she had understood a point I was making and I found her looking at me in a way that left no doubt that she had something else on her mind.

We locked eyes and stared deeply into each other's souls for what could have been ten seconds or two minutes, I have no idea. But it was an experience I will never forget. There was a sense of peace, recognition of mutual desire, respect and admiration for the other as a human being and a shared sense of how wonderful it would be to unite our souls in pleasing each other physically.

It would have been so easy, natural and I am sure enjoyable for both of us to proceed to the next step. I'd like to say it was my moral compass that pointed me away, but more likely, it was a fear of complicating my life. I am a terrible liar and would never be able to hide the truth from my wife.

The fact that I still carry this memory so vividly is testimony to my sense that the union of our souls captured in that look was better than the physical act of sex itself. Our shared intimacy left us both with a wonderful memory, a respect for the other and the peace of mind that comes from doing the right thing. In retrospect, it is as if completion of the physical act would have sullied the purity and depth of the intimacy we had shared.

# Thoughts On Soulful Connection

## Beyond The Curtain

1. Alone
2. I Am
3. The Piper

## Alone

When I am gone will they say,
I touched their soul,
They knew me well,
I understood them at their core,
They loved me in all my imperfection?

I wish it were so.
I long for that closeness
Two humans,
One soul.

There is a yearning in my heart
To be known,
Loved for who I am.
Where do I find the closeness
I seek?

Is it beyond the human experience,
A chimera of dreams,
Eternal spring of wish and desire
Outside the realm of human possibility?

Is that our fate?
Forever solitary,
Orbiting, freezing in the emptiness of space,
Mere specs of passing light.

Is there no comfort
Of knowing at our core-
We are known,
We are loved?

# Alone

*Pain comes, not from the events of our lives, but from our resistance to those events.*
— Unknown

I never liked this poem. In my opinion, it is full of overused, even hackneyed, phrases that communicate shallowness. But after many months, I found the poem began to send a chill through me. I began to feel the fear and isolation felt by the poet. The very shallowness of the words revealed the degree of isolation to which the writer is alienated from his own soul, the true source of his inspiration.

After 35 years of marriage, my wife and I divorced. Although something of a shock, in retrospect, I give Lynn credit for having the courage to act on what we both knew was a situation in which neither of us was thriving. To spend the rest of our lives in unhappiness out of habit and inertia was not the way either of us wanted to experience our last years.

My situation was complicated by the fact that I had been diagnosed with Parkinson's disease eight years earlier. The possibility of being without a caregiver as my condition deteriorated, and the idea of dying alone in some nursing home brought me face-to-face with genuine fear. Dying alone in an institution seemed like the ultimate measure of my failure as a human being. The loneliness underlying that fear was what I intended to capture in the poem. Instead, I seem to have captured my fear of loneliness.

In my 20s and early 30s, I lived alone and happily so. But after 35 years of companionship, of friends dropping by and youthful energy from children playing, I found returning to bachelorhood a lonely affair.

Even during my married years, I had few close friends of my own. Most of my outside relationships were as part of a couple or were limited to a particular activity like business, golf or serving on church committees. I suspect I was not much different from many other men who live relatively solitary lives when it comes to real intimacy beyond the home.

On one level, I found I missed the simple things like dinner conversation or sitting in the family room talking about a movie, TV show or book I was reading. I missed the presence of another human being who, by simply being there, reminded me I was alive and recognized.

On a deeper level however, I missed what I hadn't had for years, a truly intimate relationship of friendship, respect and love. This is not to put the blame on Lynn, as I am sure I did not meet her needs and I contributed equally to the problems that ultimately drove us apart.

Finding myself alone brought into full perspective the importance of fully knowing and being known by another human being, someone with whom I could share my triumphs and my defeats and who accepted me in either case. We all need someone to laugh with, to cry with, to share experiences and opinions.

Perhaps I yearn for some idealized notion of what a loving relationship can be. All is never perfect harmony between two humans. But I know that there can be those moments when two beings share at the level of their soul, when they look into each other's eyes and understand exactly who they are, thrilled by the privilege of being together in spirit. This is the comfort I seek.

## I Am

I am home.
Soaring peaks, plunging valleys,
Groaning glaciers
Call forth my soul
In tears of joy.

It seems a contradiction,
My insignificance among
The mountain majesty,
Freeing my soul from its
prison of fears.

I am home.
I am one
I am.

## I Am

*Only when your consciousness is totally focused on the moment you are in can you receive whatever gift, lesson, or delight that moment has to offer.*
—Barbara De Angelis

In the summer of 2011, I traveled with Lynn and another couple, our good friends, to Switzerland. We stayed for a few days with the family of an au pair who had worked for our friends when their children were young.

One day we took a cable car to a ridge high above the village where we were staying. We stood on the ridge covered with Lupine and other Alpine flowers. To the South, hidden behind the shoulder of the mountain on which we stood, was the upper Rhone Valley and beyond that we could see the Matterhorn rising above the surrounding mountains. Immediately to the North, we looked into a deep valley where a large glacier slowly ground its way down from the backside of the Jung Frau and Eiger peaks that fed the glacier. Surrounded by this grandeur, I was overcome with a sense of awe at the beauty and wonder of creation and of my own insignificance. In a most profound way, I felt at home, I felt at one with the world around me and I was acutely aware of the joy of my existence as a human being.

*I am home. I am one. I am.* Three simple phrases that, for me, seem to take me to a deeper, more intimate place. Home certainly is a place where I belong, where I feel safe, where I can be myself without pretense or fear, where I can shed the armor of socialization I carry into the world outside. And yes, like many people, for much of my life I shared that home with another human being, my wife. Perhaps that is why even in the safety of our homes, we often reserve a sacred personal space. For me, it is a man-cave, if you will, where only I exist.

*I am one*, not in the sense that I disappear by merging with the world about me, but one, in the sense that I belong. I am part of a unity called creation. I am as much a part of the mountain glory as the lupine that cover the ridge on which I am standing, or the glacier whose groans bear witness to its movement down the valley towards its own extinction. To feel that I am created just as the magnificence that surrounds me is created, fills me with awe and wonder. It penetrates to my soul, as if I am in the presence of the Creator himself, or at least as close to the Creator as one can get this side of death.

There is a difference between my surroundings and me. Only my fellow human beings and I are aware of the magnificence of creation. Only we feel the joy in the awareness of our own creation. That awareness raises all the fundamental questions of why, how, and who, questions that offer the possibility of a joy beyond imagination, the joy of reunion with the Creator. In this sense, the magnificence that surrounds me gives meaning to my existence, to the "I am" of life, a kind of context for my soul.

*I am* speaks to my consciousness, my awareness of who I am and where I stand in God's creation relative to other life forms, relative to other humans and relative to the Creator himself. I am reminded of the Old Testament scene where Moses sees a burning bush that is not consumed by the flames. As he approaches the bush, Moses hears the voice of God. When Moses asks God what name he should be called, God answers "*I am*".

By choosing to be called *I am*, it is as if God were telling Moses that he, God, is the ultimate awareness, the source of all knowledge in the universe. Perhaps he is also telling Moses that the special relationship between God and humans is centered on our human capacity for awareness of self and of others in God's creation and that we draw closer to God by increasing our awareness of creation and of God's hope for the future of his creation.

*I am* also brings to mind the vision of a newborn baby, coated in its white birthing cream, looking up in wonder at its new existence with all its yet un-sensed possibilities. What is different now from a few hours before when it was still safely floating in that dark sanctum of its mother's womb? Was there an "I am" then? Does its newfound separateness create its essence, its soul? Is this the soul that will exist for its entire lifetime or will it change as it rubs up against the engraver's wheel that is life?

I suppose the soul is brought into existence by our own consciousness, by our awareness that we exist as separate from other souls. I am unique and therefore *I am.*

But do I exist when I am asleep and unconscious of my surroundings? Of course I do. Is not my birthing just my first awakening? If so, when did my "I am" enter into what was to become my physical self? Does our soul emerge with time as cells multiply and specialize forming infant hearts, lungs, brains and, perhaps, awareness? Perhaps our birth is just one of many mile posts in our journey through life as our soul evolves from nothingness to consciousness of self, to awareness of creation and, if we are fortunate, to enlightenment.

I am hopeful that when I die my soul will leave my physical body to rejoin with our Creator. Many who have had near death experiences talk of such wonders. I hope it is true, but also recognize that the brain, in all of its wonder, can create its own reality in our subconscious dreams as well as in our conscious imaginings. Death is life's last great adventure.

# The Piper

The sound of pipes pierces the mist
Bringing to mind the olden days
Emerging through the fog of time
Awakening my soul to those gone by.

What hidden memories deep within
Awakened by the piper's din
Call me forth in brotherhood
To learn from them what I could.

What secrets lie hidden within
Of lives and loves of my kin
The piper brings them all to life
And shields me from my current strife.

That sense of one with persons past
Brings me to a deeper place
Where fears and tears of modern days
Yield to knowing--- I'm OK.

A line of love leads the way
Connecting me with ancient days
My soul now knows my future rests
In hands of those long since passed.

And when I too join that line
Of pipers past playing through time
I'll speak to those who follow me
Through the mist of unconscious being.

How we know what we know
When we free ourselves of struggle
We enter into the mists of time
To know the secrets of that line.

# The Piper

*I hope it is true that a man can die and yet not only live in others but give them life, and not only life, but that great consciousness of life.*
—Jack Kerouac

The Inn at Spanish Bay in Pacific Grove, California has a bag piper play every evening at sunset. I visited there on New Year's Day when it was cool but clear. As the sun sank to the horizon, a mist formed over the golf course. From that mist emerged the sound of a piper playing as he approached the patio where I sat. As the piper approached, I could see he was dressed in full Scottish regalia, the tartan kilt, black buckled shoes, heavy white calf length stockings, an open white shirt and a tartan cap.

There's a primitive, even mournful, quality to the sound of the bagpipes. The piper emerging from the mist lent an eerie, ghost-like feeling to the occasion. I had an overwhelming sense of being witness to a long line of pipers going back through time. I felt they were there to help me with their experience and, most of all, comfort me with their sense of continuity.

We are all part of a long line of souls whose collective wisdom has much to teach us. In some small way we have elements of generations past in our genetic makeup as well as in the social values and memes that are passed from generation to generation through example, through letters and stories and through wisdom shared over evening meals.

To a large extent this historical legacy defines who we are as human beings. Just as genes tell birds how, when and where to migrate, our inherited genes and learned values provide a compass of inner knowing that lies mostly hidden in the mists of our unconscious. These inner guideposts are a truly rewarding gift to those who make the effort to seek them out.

In my busy, high-energy world, it is not easy to make time to find the quiet and inspirational atmosphere I need to help me access my inner knowing. I find it most helpful to set aside a specific time each day, my sacred time if you will, to quiet the inner voices that bombard my conscious mind with "to-dos", "shoulds,"and other messages seeking my attention. My quiet time creates the space for my inner knowing to emerge to remind me who I am, what I stand for and where my inner compass is pointing. It settles my spirit and provides a kind of moral direction, keeping me on course as I re-enter the everyday world.

That I am part of a continuum that extends through generations into ancient times comforts me. Yes, there is comfort in knowing I live on, not just for a generation or two in someone's memory, but as wisdom and knowledge that gets passed on to new generations. It's as if I leave something behind that makes the earth a better place and improves the human condition for those who follow. Our lives are not for naught. Even after death we are needed by those who listen for the wisdom from pipers past.

# Thoughts On Beyond The Curtain

# Afterword

I started this book with a statement of my ordinariness. Looking back over what I have written, I see all the emotions present in any ordinary life, joy, love, grace and shared intimacy as well as anger, loneliness, regret and a sense of failure. I suspect we all experience these emotions at some point in our lives.

From a literary standpoint, it would be nice, I suppose, to end this book with some kind of inspirational breakthrough where in one transforming moment I manage to free myself from the limitations of my own humanity and live out my life bathed in an aura of love. This has not happened, nor do I think it will. Life does not operate like that except in very rare instances. My life, for sure, has been much more incremental.

It may not be as exciting as some transforming Big Bang, but I find hope and reason to go on in pursuing a more soul-filled life even if it is in small increments. In reviewing what I have written, I see personal growth and a deepening of my life experience. Yes, it has taken many years, and perhaps, I might have accomplished more had I been more aware. But in that deepening process, I know I have become more alive, closer to my essence, closer to my fellow human beings and closer to my Creator. For me, it is no small accomplishment just to be able to experience these feelings.

No doubt there is more to be written. I see a significant hole in the absence of a poem about my mother as well as one about Lynn. Given the major role these women have played in my life, this absence is telling. I keep working at it and wait patiently for the muse to return giving voice to words of healing and closure. I know they are there, somewhere inside, waiting to be freed.

If I have any regrets, it is only that I was not more aware sooner. Increased awareness may have allowed me to make better choices, avoiding many of my mistakes. When I look at my mistakes and lack of awareness, I see a pattern of unwillingness to deal with the negatives in my life in a timely manner. It is understandable. We are most successful in our relationships with others and with ourselves when we are positive and supportive, when we respond with kindness, compassion and grace, when we show love and respect. But we learn the most when we examine our negative behaviors. We need to savor our successes if only to keep us excited and motivated by the rewards of a rich life experience. We also need to examine, learn from and correct our failures so we can move ever closer to a rich, soulful life.

At this point in my life, I try to keep an awareness of both my positives and my negatives in front of me as I live each day. This is not easy. It requires effort and discipline. To aid me in my efforts, I set aside some time each day to review the truths about my own life journey as follows:

1. *My soul is the Divine presence at the very center of my being.* To keep awareness of that divine presence front and center in my life, I try to experience it every day.

2. *Fear is a constant presence in my life; deal with it.* I ask myself what fears are operating today. I go toward my fear by peeling away the layers of rationalization and excuses that surround it. I know I have arrived at my true fear when the rationalizations and excuses cease focusing on others and are centered on me.

3. *I am judgmental.* Where is my judgment creating distance in my life? What fear lies behind my judgment?

4. *I am love!* If I want to experience that love, I must give it away in all my interactions, be they with someone close to me or with the checkout lady at the grocery store.

# Appendix

The following questions are provided for those readers who may be looking for assistance in expanding their thinking about their own life experience. These questions may also be helpful in structuring a conversation with a partner or others in a small group discussion. Specific questions may or may not be relevant to an individual reader.

I.     The Innocence Of Childhood
   - As a child, where did you go to find quiet and comfort?
   - What childhood experiences underlie or influence your spiritual life as an adult?
   - What do you believe Jesus meant when he said we must become as little children if we are to enter the Kingdom of Heaven?

II.    My Shadow Side
   - How would you describe your shadow side?
   - How does your shadow side impact your life?
   - What makes you angry in your personal relationships?
   - Can you tie your anger back to an experience you might have had as a child?
   - How would you describe your Big Me and Little Me?
   - What prevents you from living your Big Me all the time?

III.   My Inward Journey
   - Are there examples from your life where you initiated major change as opposed to having change thrust upon you?

- Where do you see yourself on the journey from self awareness, to self acceptance and self love?
- How could your emotional and spiritual life be more satisfying?
- In what way does fear prevent you from achieving the emotional and spiritual life you desire?
- In what way is judgment of others restricting your emotional life?
- What incremental steps can you take toward achieving your vision of a more satisfying emotional and spiritual life?

IV.    Soulful Connection
- Where in your life are you the most creative?
- Who in your life needs more of your love? What can you do to show more love? Is there anything in your attitude toward this person that you need to change?
- Is there anyone in your life from whom you need to feel more love? Is there anything in your attitude toward this person that may be preventing their showing you more love? How can you communicate your need to this person with loving kindness?
- What expressions of love and gratitude do you hold in your heart for someone close to you but are afraid to express? What fear keeps you from expressing your feelings?

V.    Beyond The Curtain
- To what degree are inherited behaviors or deeply ingrained social memes operating in your life?
- Describe a time when you felt most connected to the Creator.

- How would you describe the Creator?
- What is your understanding of the human soul?
- Is the soul the same or different from human consciousness?
- What is your view of birth, death and the human soul?

VI.  Afterword
- What would be your personal meditation if you were to meditate daily?